rejUvenation

Becoming a Better You

rejUvenation

Published by Jus King Publications

Chicago, IL.

Cover design by Open Mic Production

Printed in the United States of America.

Acknowledgements

What would an acknowledgement page be without giving glory and praises to the Most High? Thank you, God, for being my guiding light. I would like to thank my children: Aaron, Jasmine, and Josiah. You guys mean the world to me and I cherish each one of you. Thank you, Kevin, my love, for always supporting my movements. Mama, I appreciate you for everything you have ever done and continuously do for me. I love you. To those who purchased my first book and encouraged me to keep going, I say thank you. To my fellow podcasters, Wesley and Shawntia, looking fabulous on my cover page.... thanks y'all! Last, but certainly not least, thank each and every one of you who purchased this book. I hope that it serves as a guide to you becoming the person you desperately desire to be. Thank you!!!

PREFACE

Often times, you may find yourself stuck, not knowing how to fulfill your passion. You may fool around with the idea, but never put it into motion. You then begin to settle because, somehow, you have convinced yourself that doing what you love is not going to put food on the table or a roof over your head. Time goes by, and before you know it, you are still where you were years ago. Why? Because you have allowed yourself to get in your own way.

When I first contemplated writing a book, I quickly shut down the idea. I did so because I was inexperienced and clueless. I thought many times, "Who am I kidding? I'm no author." I knew I wanted to write, but I didn't know how to begin, nor did I understand how to go about publishing or editing. So, I pushed the idea into the back of my head and it stayed there for years.

Failed relationships, lack of loyalty from those around me, a somewhat fatherless household, single motherhood, not accepting myself for who I was, hating my body image; these are just some of many issues that haunted me throughout my life. These are the things I allowed to keep me from being a better version of myself. I kept thinking, "Am I the only person to feel this way? I can't be. There has to be others out there that share my same struggles."

As days, months, and years passed by, I worked jobs here and there, dabbled with schooling, and continued taking care of my kids. Most times, I found myself living check to check. And although I knew I was blessed to obtain employment throughout the years, I still felt like something was missing. I wasn't satisfied. I was unhappy, in a sense. I would be at work thinking about everything except work. But the one thing I always found myself doing was writing. I would jot down whatever I was feeling at the moment, the things that upset me, the things I wanted for my children and myself. And although it took almost two long decades, I realized it was time to do what I had always desired. It was then that I picked up a pen and notebook and started writing. Thoughts were formulating faster than I could write them down. Love, relationships, loyalty, toxicity, and so many more thoughts overcrowded my head. And having the knowledge that I have on these matters meant nothing if I could not share it with those out there like myself.

Unlike any tools of survival that were given to me, I want to share my experiences with you because these are situations that enter our lives on a daily basis. How do you deal with acknowledgment from others without losing yourself? How do you handle negative, toxic family and friends? How do you love again after continuously being betrayed? How do you plan for your future without compromising your present? How do you take care of your kids and chase your dreams at the same time? How do you push through your pain? How do you physically, mentally, and emotionally accept yourself for who you are? How do you continue to be a pillar for others without losing yourself? How do you take control of your life?

I embarked on my hidden desire. I gave birth to my passion for writing. And so I commenced, as will you. With every sentence that you read, you will begin to understand more about yourself than ever before. You will love yourself, admire yourself, and become one with yourself. You will venture out into the world and become unstoppable. You will make a name for yourself. You will become a better you!

Table Of Contents

Chapter One

Alpha

I. Getting Started

II. Going Back in Time

I.

There is an issue, on a universal level, that people unknowingly share. It is one of our biggest contributors to our failures for success. It preys on the strong and the weak. It has limitless boundaries. It doesn't discriminate and we all have succumbed to this terrible thing: Procrastination.

Procrastination is the reason why you haven't made that doctor's appointment, even though you've been coughing up a lung for the past three weeks. It is the reason why you haven't applied for Cosmetology school, in spite of the fact that you've been doing hair since you were twelve years old. It is the reason why you haven't enrolled in college, although you are only two credits away from having a degree. It's the reason why you are still in a hopeless, dead relationship, despite the signs given to you months ago. It is the reason why you are on your third pack of your "last" pack of cigarettes. And it is the reason why you have yet to join your 24-hour neighborhood gym, seeing as how you get off work at 5:00pm every day of the week.

In order for your life to begin anew, you must first break your vicious cycle of procrastination. And in order to do so, you must be willing to admit that you are a procrastinator. Once you have admitted to yourself that you are the person you do not wish to be, it is then that you can begin the process of evolving into the person that you yearn to become.

For as long as I can remember, I had always postponed the thought of being a writer. I was only a little girl. What did I know about formulating a complete sentence? I had not even been introduced to adjectives, conjunctions, and every other bit of English terminology you can think of. All I knew was that I relished the feel of a writing utensil in my hand. I loved jotting down a bunch of words that made absolutely no sense. I carried those feelings with me for years.

While my elementary school teachers were drilling the thought of becoming doctors and lawyers in everyone else's heads, I silently thought, "What's wrong with writing?" Nothing was wrong with it. But coming up in my era, we were persuaded to establish careers that came with a guaranteed check, a career that was sure to take care of you and your family, financially.

As a child, it is almost impossible to understand the magnitude of exactly where your passion can take you because this world is so driven by money. Sometimes, when we are fixated on the wrong things, we tend to lose sight of who we are as a whole. It carries over into different aspects of our lives: love, loyalty, health, relationships, friendships, goals, and even respect. Am I saying it is not okay to want to make money? Absolutely not. What I am saying is it is not okay to be so busy making money that you forget who and what is significant in your life, one of those factors being you. There has to be a balance.

In order to better yourself, you must get to the root of the problem. You have to identify the issues you encounter on a daily basis, decide what it is that you want to fix, dedicate yourself to fixing it, and empower the next individual to do the same. It's a cycle. We need to uplift one another, but we must first improve ourselves.

We spend so much time on frivolous things without understanding the negative impact it is having on us becoming better individuals. We set goals in our minds and let time pass without ever really trying to reach those goals. Again, this stems from procrastination.

How many times have you analyzed your existence and thought to yourself, "This can't be my purpose. This can't be life." You get up, go to work, and go home. Before you know it, the day is gone, yet you haven't accomplished anything that will benefit you. You lie in bed and think to yourself for so long, hours have lapsed. While you are driving, you are thinking so hard, you've reached your destination without even realizing it. You shower, and while letting the water trickle down your body, you are wondering, "When will things get better for me?" Things will not get better until you make them better. Easier said than done, right?

Nothing worth having comes easy. Develop plans and put them into motion.

Ask yourself, "What do I want for myself? What are my goals? What do I want to change about my daily living?" Once you have asked yourself these things, come up with answers. If you do not have answers, there is no way you can begin to change.

Jot your answers down and begin to work on your missions daily. The key to reaching goals is knowing that nothing happens overnight. For example, if you want to change your eating habits, begin the process by removing unhealthy foods from your diet, a few at a time. If you remove everything at once, there is a chance you may get discouraged, which can result in failure. Whatever goals you set for yourself, strive for them in moderation. There is no hurry. The ultimate objective is to be a better person than you were the day before.

During your journey of becoming a better you, you must prioritize. There should be some goals that take precedence over others. For example, if your goal is to own your own business, yet you are in debt, you must work toward getting yourself out of debt before pursuing plans of entrepreneurship.   It will be easy to get off track if you do not prioritize. Do not work backwards. Set up an orderly agenda, one with expected times/dates of task deadlines and completions, and one that flows with your life and your goals.

Once you have begun this process, you must stick with it. Consistency will make or break your journey, for it is key to succeeding. Do not waste precious time and energy on unimportant matters. Although it will be extremely challenging, you must remain disciplined and focused. There are days where you will contemplate quitting. But during those times, you must fight. You must dig deep down inside and find the strength to prevail. Think not only of yourself, but also of those who may be affected by the outcomes, or lack thereof. Think of why you started in the first place.

If you find difficulty in motivating yourself, try a few tactics to help you stay on track. Compose a chart, writing on it all of your goals you intend on reaching week by week. Once you reach each goal, scratch it off and celebrate your victory. Remember, a victory is a victory, whether big or small.

Seeing is believing, right? If possible, post a picture of your goal. Have this picture in each place of your home where you spend the most time. Look at the picture and remind yourself that you will reach that goal without letting anyone or anything get in your way.

Remember, it is no one else's job to improve your life. That is your responsibility. When setting goals, be realistic. Do not set a goal you know you cannot achieve in a given time. Do not overexert yourself trying to achieve many goals in a short time frame. There is no rush, hence the reason for your feasible deadlines.

While it is great to receive encouragement from those around you, do not expect it. If you have a support system, be appreciative of that. Yes, getting that extra push from people will make you strive to do better and go harder. But if you expect it, yet do not receive it, it is easy to lose focus and fall off track. You must learn to be your own motivator. After all, it is about bettering yourself first. We are no good to others if we are no good to ourselves. We cannot truly help others if we lack the knowledge and experience ourselves.

In any given situation, you must learn to be your own best friend. Treat yourself how you would treat someone you love. You would not down talk your mother, so why do it to yourself? Be kind to yourself instead of being so judgmental. Support your own goals and aspirations. Put yourself first, not because you are selfish, but because you understand that this is the first step to being selfless. Make time in the day for you, whatever that may consist of. Stay positive, reward yourself, and take care of yourself. Once again, celebrate every victory, whether big or small. You deserve it.

You may not be where you want to be in life. And yes, there may be an explanation for it. However, you must own up to your mistakes and drawbacks. It is easy to point the blame at someone else for your shortcomings. Sometimes, you may even find yourself critiquing other peoples' lives. Nonetheless, when you spend time looking for faults in others, you leave no time to correct your own. When you blame others, you give up your own power to grow. You will never excel in your life if you are sitting back waiting for others to fail. When you pray for someone's downfall, you are relinquishing your power to succeed.

Discover the type of person you yearn to become. Dig deep down into your soul, and with every fiber of your being, tell yourself, "I got this!" Wake up everyday with a new perspective on life. Get out of bed with a mission in mind. Stay focused and keep your eyes on the prize, knowing that you will succeed in becoming a better you.

II.

You may be stuck, saying to yourself, "I want to begin, but I don't know how. Where do I start?" Start from the very beginning, as far back as you can remember. Go back to your childhood. Close your eyes and exhume old memories from your mind. For some, this may bring unwanted recollections. For others, it may bring remembrances of joy. Whatever the case, in order to find yourself, you must go back to the original source...a younger you.

When I was a little girl, I remember a life of good times. My parents spoiled my older brother and me. We received just about anything we wanted. We would go to sleep and wake up with money underneath our pillows. We would go to school and come home to a new pair of gym shoes in our rooms. We would receive the latest and greatest of everything: scooters, bikes, and even the best radio and gaming systems.

I remember one Christmas morning, while living in Chicago, on 53rd and Carpenter, we woke up to a living room filled with gifts. There were so many, my parents could not wrap them all. Nor could they fit all the gifts underneath the Christmas tree. So, they lined them up against the living room walls and on top of our couches. We loved living in this home. It held memories we could never forget.

There was always a hot meal waiting for us. My mother was actively involved in every aspect of our lives. She would help out at our schools by volunteering. Being a seamstress, amongst many other things, she would even make our Halloween costumes for competitions taking place at our school. One year, she made my brother a Captain Hook costume, while I was the Statue of Liberty. We won first and second place. She sewed together our Easter outfits, making outfits for some of my cousins as well. Life was great. Carpenter Street was fantastic. We had many friends. We enjoyed the good times. And then we moved. And after that home, we moved to another.

Moving was the part I did not enjoy. My brother and I literally attended six different schools in six years. I could not understand why we kept moving from place to place. It saddened me every time I had to tell my friends goodbye. In my heart, I knew I would not see them again, but I held on to hope. It was not until my seventh grade year that we stopped bouncing around. Unfortunately, my mother and father separated right before then. I knew that our lives would change. I just didn't know how.

During those years of bouncing around, I always wrote. I felt like I just wanted to share my thoughts with my journal. Anytime I had something on my heart and mind, I pulled out my pen and paper and wrote down how I was feeling. I was not good at discussing how I felt with others. I was very shy and reserved. I enjoyed being able to release my feelings through journaling. It was like a weight being lifted off of my shoulders. No matter what was going on, I was always writing about it. In turn, I knew I was destined to become a writer.

Think back to your childhood. What do you remember? What hurt you the most? What wonderful memories do you have? As much as it may pain you to recollect, you must do so in order to know and understand how this has played a part in the person you are today. You may have been someone who grew up in a drug-infested household. You may have seen things you wish you could erase from your memory. During your childhood, what did you go through that made you decide to take the path you did? Good or bad, what did you take away from your childhood that can help you transpire into the person you yearn to become? The answer lies in you. Only you can find it.

Many people become powerless because they let their past define them. Do not transform into that person. Your past does not define you, but only mold you into the person you do or do not want to be. The time for blaming your past on your present life is over. Your past can no longer be an excuse for your actions today because where you are today is a result of the previous choices you made. Unfortunately, you cannot alter your past, but you do not have to be controlled by it either. In order to have better, you must do better. The power to change your life is in your hands. The time for fretting is over. In order to change your circumstances, you must alter how you look at them. Live by the three R's: **R**eview, **R**evise, and **R**epeat. Review your life thus far, taking notice of every aspect you are choosing to modify. Revise your daily living by working on those aspects in need of modification. Repeat any steps necessary to uphold your revisions.

Some people channel their anger and turn it into something positive, while others need a bit of guidance. Whatever has angered you, whatever memories of your childhood you have that may have impacted you negatively can be reversed. You have to find it in yourself and have the will to say, "I will not let the pain of my past defeat me. I am destined to become the person I want to be. No one can choose my fate because I am in control of my life." Say this to yourself, as many times as it takes, and believe it with everything you have. You do not have to become a victim of circumstance. You hold the pen. No one can write your story but you. Yes, you may have gone through hard times. Always look at what you have left. Never focus on what you've lost. It's not what happened to you. It's what you do about it. We only have one life. There are no do-overs. It is time to live life right. If something is not right, fix it. If you are destined to become something, make it happen. If you are not happy with your path, walk a different one. It is not too late. Start today.

Chapter Two

Self-love, Self-Acceptance

I. Love the Skin You're In

II. Damages of Stress

I.

After speaking with many women and asking what were a few things that mattered most, one thing was pretty much the same: love. Women want to be adored. We want the same love that we put out. We want to be seen as beautiful by our mate, and we want to be told. We want to be appreciated and not taken for granted. We want someone who matches our drive. We want many things. But do we understand that the things we want start with us?

Men also want the feeling of love to be reciprocated. They want to feel like they matter. They yearn for attention as well. They need to feel like they are the providers. They need to feel respected.

In order to want love, you must ask yourself what love means to you. For some, love means showing affection more often than not. It means spoiling you and showering you with the best. Maybe it means to be as one, on a spiritual level. Or it could also mean waking up to a rose and a love note on your nightstand. Whatever your definition of love is, you must be completely willing to give exactly what it is you expect.

As mentioned before, everything you yearn for in life starts with you. Having said that, you cannot expect your mate to see you as beautiful or handsome if you don't see it yourself. You have to appreciate all of your imperfections and wear them proudly. Be so confident with your flaws that others cannot use them to insult you. Because the minute you allow your imperfections to make you feel anything less than appealing, you have just given yourself permission to become victim to someone who will do just the same.

How do you love the skin you're in? Accept yourself. Acknowledge who you are and who you are not. If you are 5'2", come to terms with the fact that you will never be 5'6", as it is just not possible to achieve that specific desire. Boost your confidence by achieving self-acceptance.

Increasing your self-acceptance will come easier for some than it will for others. Before you begin on your road to self-improvement, you must understand that you need to make these changes for you, and only you. Whatever reasons you have for wanting to take this venture should have nothing to do with the opinions of another individual. It should not be because Johnny thinks your thighs are too big, or because Tammy said your hair is too kinky. Men, it shouldn't be because Kristen feels like you should cut your beard, or because her mother thinks you should work out more. Recognize that this journey has zero to do with your outer shell, but more so accepting and loving yourself for the beautiful person you are.

When I was younger, I hated my big forehead, wide nose, and full lips. And then there was this green vein that sometimes protruded out the side of my forehead. I was short and skinny with a high butt. There was no way I would put on a dress and expose my chicken legs. I used to wonder why I was cursed with particularly three bad features. Why not just the big forehead? Why did I have to have the nose and lips to match? Because I felt this way about my strong features, it would hurt my feelings when people would talk about them. As much as I would try to ignore it, a part of me agreed with it.

Entering high school, I looked like I was fresh out of fifth grade. Nothing about me screamed mature. I looked as if I did not belong. Other girls around me seemed so developed and ready for high school life, while I was still trying to figure out how I would fit in. I was never a makeup kind of girl, nor did I carry a purse. Still shy, I walked into each class as if I was ready for it to be over. The only thing I kept thinking was just how long the next four years would be for me.

Being in Honors classes allowed me to feel a little more at peace. There were people in my classes I could relate to on a social level. I ended up meeting two girls, Nicole and Kelly, who would become my best friends. Ironically, we were completely different, yet one in the same. Kelly was the cool, popular kid. Nicole was a bit more reserved, but she showed her character through her laugh and personality. We latched on to one another. The more they began to know me, the more intrigued they were by me.

One day after school, we went to Nicole's house. They gave me a slight hair makeover, completely out of boredom. I always wore my hair in a ponytail, so they decided to change that. After they washed, flat ironed, and styled my hair, I felt like a different person. Once I saw myself in the mirror, I began to realize that I could step out of my comfort zone, change my looks a bit, and still be myself.

The older I became, the more I realized I was beautiful in my own way. This forehead wasn't going anywhere! And neither were my lips nor nose. So I began to pull my hair off my face and expose my beautiful imperfections. It was nothing anyone could say about my forehead that would make me revert to hiding it again. While I was so busy hating my big lips in my younger years, I had no idea that there were others who had wished for them.

Once I started feeling beautiful, I felt a sense of relief. I felt like a different person, a better person. One half of me was mad because it took so long to accept myself, while the other half was just grateful that I did.

I'm sure you have things about yourself that you wish you could change. However, change is not possible because these are the attributes God has rewarded you with. So, what now? You wear it with complete confidence. If your goal is to lose weight, then by all means set up a regimen to do so. And do it for you. Convince yourself and believe that you are attractive as you are. Then begin the process by telling yourself that your weight loss goal is about improving your health and self-confidence, not about improving your looks for the likes of others. But, until you reach the 130 pounds you desire, you better strut that 195 pounds with complete confidence! Embrace your wide, small, or slightly crooked nose. Love the gap between your teeth. Blow yourself a kiss with those bounteous or undersized lips. Adore your wide hips. Be captivated by those alluring clusters of freckles on your face and torso. Wear your surgery scar proudly. Hold your head up high over your successfully performed mastectomy. Own up to your body and dare not let another's negative feelings about your physical attributes have any bearing on your confidence. Flatter yourself instead of seeking the approval of others. Instead of thinking you have to change, change the thought of thinking that you have to change. Conform to no one's expectations but your own. Remember, self-love is the best love.

Men, you are not exempt! Love the physique God gave you. Strut with confidence as well. Do not look at the next man in the gym and try to become him. Be confident that your body is just that.... YOUR body. Understand that your body structure is not the same as his. Love your beer belly instead of envying his six-pack. Be okay with not being a part of the "beard gang." Fall in love with your constantly growing cluster of gray hairs. If the person you desire does not like your nappy roots, then guess what? That's not the person for you!

Self-acceptance is not only good for your well-being, but it is also important for everyday living. You begin to understand more about your strengths versus your weaknesses, which will allow you to have the courage to face all adversities. You learn to appreciate yourself, thus demanding those around you to do just the same. You gain a sense of self-understanding. You have a newfound self-respect.

One exercise you can utilize, in order to achieve the self-love and self-acceptance you desire, is to pull out a pen and paper and write down all of the things you love about yourself versus the things you are not so crazy about. You can try sticky notes as well. Create a "self-acceptance" wall in your room, office, or anywhere you see fit. Once you have written these things down, go over your list, or your wall of sticky notes, and see if the good dominates the bad. If it does, you are already off to a good start. If not, do not worry.

For those times you are having a not so good moment, go to your list and look at the good attributes you have written down about yourself. For example, if your tall height begins to bother you, look at your list and choose one reason that can negate that self-conscious feeling. Say to yourself, "I am taller than most, but my height allowed me to play the position I desired in basketball. I loved playing basketball." If your big eyes are not so appealing to you, go to your list, look it over, and say to yourself, "My eyes are big, but my lashes accentuate them in a way that I love. I am pretty, regardless." Once you begin to accept those physical characteristics, cross the "bad ones" off your list. Pretty soon, the good will begin to outweigh anything negative you feel about yourself. But this can only happen if you continuously drill in your head the importance of self-acceptance and believe that you are nothing but extraordinary. After all, if you are searching for that one person who will change your life, take a look in the mirror. You will never know what it is like to experience happiness if your happiness is contingent upon the thoughts and actions of another. Again, it starts with you.

Self-acceptance is not always about the outer shell. Maybe you promised yourself years ago that, by the time you turned 30, you would have a certain amount of money saved. Or perhaps you did not reach your goal of becoming a doctor. You must accept and forgive yourself. Focus on your strengths instead of dwelling on your shortcomings. Concentrate on the present you, look forward to a bright future, and let go of the unaltered past. Accept yourself in order to improve yourself. Recognize that a life of self-love and self-acceptance is far better than a life of regrets and what-ifs. Think of all the tough times you did not succumb to. Celebrate those moments.

Once you have accepted yourself for the amazing person you are, spread that positivity to the next individual in need. Remember to empower. Help that coworker of yours to understand she is unique, and that is what makes her beautiful. Assist that janitor you see with his head down and remind him that he is no less of a person than anyone else. Let him know he is appreciated. Remind your teenage cousin that beauty comes in all different shapes and sizes. So don't worry about fitting in more so than standing out. Empower, empower, empower!

II.

Not only is it important to be comfortable in your skin, for purposes of loving yourself, it is healthier. When you put so much emphasis on trying to fit the mold or keep up with the next person's looks, you become unhealthy on a physical, mental, and emotional level. It disturbs your well-being and literally affects each of your organ systems. How so? Let us delve further.

The human body is composed of 11 systems: circulatory, respiratory, digestive, excretory, nervous, endocrine, immune, integumentary, skeletal, muscle, and reproductive. While I won't overload you with tons of information on each system, I will discuss the impact of stress on a few, starting with one of the most important...the cardiovascular system.

The cardiovascular system is one of the most significant organ systems, primarily because this is where the heart resides. Without it, we do not exist. Therefore, it is vital to keep it functioning as it should.

According to www.healthline.com, our hearts pump more rapidly during stress. "Stress hormones cause your blood vessels to constrict and raise your blood pressure." Understand that stress can come from pleasant and unpleasant situations. It is a natural body reaction. Nonetheless, when you frequently stress, you are making your heart work harder than it has to, which in turn raises your risk of having high blood pressure (hypertension). High blood pressure is known as "the silent killer." It sneaks up on you without warning. If left untreated, you are creating issues with your blood vessels, thus putting you at risk for a heart attack or a stroke.

Who would have ever thought that the muscular system could fall victim to stress? I certainly did not. I remember a few years ago like it was yesterday; I was having a bit of pain in the lower part of my neck, right between my shoulder blades. Of course, I brushed it off as having slept the wrong way. I figured it would subside. However, it did not. This pain lasted for several weeks. It became worse. It was to the point where I could hardly turn my head without pain radiating from the base of my neck to the blades of my shoulders. I finally decided enough was enough.

I sought out the advice of a doctor. I'm thinking, "Maybe I unknowingly injured myself. Or could I have a serious, underlying issue?" I was nervous. After running several tests on me, they could find nothing. Then the questions came. The more they inquired, the more I had begun to feel like the nurses and doctors were just being nosey. They even asked me if I was pregnant.

"No," I replied.

"Yes, you are," said the doctor.

I looked up, scratched the back of my aching neck, and said, "Come again?"

Yes, I was pregnant and had no idea. After consulting with the doctor, she informed me that my pain could have come from added stress. It dawned on me. At that time, it was a bit rough for my immediate family and me. I was working a job that I absolutely despised, we were financially strapped, and I was attempting to get myself back in school. It was challenging. But I knew I had a life inside of me that depended solely on me. So, I did what I had to do. I stopped stressing over the things I could not control and took hold of the things I could. Lo and behold, my neck and shoulder pain slowly faded away. I have no choice but to believe I was causing my own pain.

When you are under stress, your muscles "tense up to protect themselves from injury." If you are constantly stressed, your muscles are not given a chance to relax or recover. This, in turn, can cause many pains, including "headaches, back and shoulder pain, and body aches."

How important is your skin to you? School has taught us that skin is the largest organ of the body. The integumentary system, comprised of hair, skin, and nails is just as important as any other body system. It helps provide a barrier of protection against infections and bodily injuries. I found it very informative, after reading an article on www.sound-mind.org, just how much stress can interrupt our integumentary system's ability to help us "heal wounds properly", fight skin infections, and aid in "premature aging." If you have ever wondered why your hair and nails are so brittle, stress could be the reason. The acne on your face could be another indicator.

Last, but undoubtedly not least, if you have lost your desire to have sex, or even be sexy for your mate, stress could surely be a reason why. It tampers with your reproductive organs, lessening your libido. This, in turn, can also affect your sexual performance and make your urethra "prone to infection."

As you can see, stress is not to be taken lightly. Again, you must learn to live with, love, and accept the person you are, physically. Once you do so, you are emotionally strengthened. Your mental capacity is then at its prime. When you embrace yourself, you leave others with two options: Embrace you as well or keep it moving. You are an unyielding force of nature. Your confidence is through the roof, which will make those around you second-guess insulting you. Why? Because they know you will not be fazed. Your dazzling radiance will permeate a room. In turn, you will be able to uplift the next individual. Remember, it is all about empowerment.

Soldiers have a creed, whereas they vow to never leave a fallen soldier behind. We need to have that same approach. Love one another enough to help build each other up. Do not be so caught up in yourself that you cannot serve as a mentor for the next person in need. Elevate your fellow brothers and sisters.

Chapter Three

Relationships

I. Companions

II. Children

III. Parents

IV. Friends

I.

Another matter that is important to women is relationships. Relationships can be a very touchy subject. We meet someone, consistently spend time together, have great sex followed by cuddling sessions, possibly have a child or two, and then it's over. The time is no longer being spent, you are becoming more and more disengaged, sex is at a bare minimum, and before you know it, you two have gone your separate ways. You, then, begin to bombard yourself with the questions. Why didn't you two work out? You replay everything in your head, but nothing seems to make sense. You cry, pout, and become bitter. Trying to gain an understanding, you call your best friend to tell her you are coming over. Once you arrive, you begin to bash your ex to your friend. You two gossip about it as the day comes to an end. And when you go home, you relive those sad, hurtful moments in your head all over again. Here you are, having another restless night.

Relationships are just as important to men. They need to feel like the provider. They thrive off making their partner happy. Unlike women,

men are not overly emotional. However, they desire to have their abilities and efforts recognized. And when they aren't, it makes them feel like a part of their needs are not being achieved. Guys deal with heartaches several different ways: drinks with their boys, cutting off contact, getting sexually involved with someone else, or even being a complete asshole.

One of the biggest failures of relationships is not being completely honest from the beginning. When initially meeting, it is very crucial that you set boundaries and expectations. Lots of time is wasted in relationships because people enter them, not having a clear understanding of what their mate is actually looking for. If you are seeking a long-term, committed relationship, do not be afraid to voice your requirement. If this is not what the other party is looking for, you have just saved both of you a great deal of senseless heartache and pain. Sit down and talk about your futures, wants, and desires. Lay it on the table before you lay in the bed. Do not be afraid to delve further into your potential mate's life rather than settling on their superficial qualities.

Sadly enough, plenty of women believe they can reel someone in based off of their physical attributes. Go ahead and doll yourself up. Put on your best pair of Red Bottoms. Squirm into those expensive pair of fitted jeans with the dazzling top to match. Wear that Victoria's Secret push up bra and make the "girls" sit extra pretty. Beat that face like it's no tomorrow. And don't forget to grab that Louis Vuitton clutch on the way out. Guess what? If your partner does not want to be with you, it simply will not happen. It is perfectly fine to look gorgeous, as long as you know and understand what you are getting yourself into. No matter what you do or how you do it, commitment will not happen unless your companion is ready.

The same goes for men. Sure, your chest looks great in that tight, white T-shirt, right along with your bulging biceps. Yes, you have the flyest whip in town. Oh, you own your own barber shop? Okay! Looking good in those gray sweatpants! You got a wad of money in your pocket? Awesome! Yet, it still means nothing if that person you desire isn't ready.

Women are emotional creatures by nature. But we all are our own worst critics. As mentioned before, we must love ourselves and accept all of our imperfections. If you have not done so, refrain from entering a relationship because your insecurities will carry over into it. Do not make your partner suffer because of your uncertainties. Doubting yourself will cause you to formulate all of these false scenarios in your head. You will suddenly have the answer as to why you have yet to receive a text back, or why it is 6:32pm and you are still sitting on the couch, with your arms folded, waiting for the front door to open. In essence, you will drive yourself crazy concocting preposterous stories.

To know your partner is to understand your partner. If you do not know the wants of this person you lay next to every night, how can you expect it to last? Furthermore, you must also know yourself. Do not expect for your mate to be something you are not. The time to find yourself is not while you are in a relationship. You cannot expect someone to stick around while you are still trying to figure it all out. Once you have invested in yourself, it is then that you can invest in the needs of others.

Having said so, be mindful of the fact that a relationship is a two-way street. Ask yourself, "What am I bringing to the table besides good looks and great sex?" You require your potential lover to have goals, make money, be family-oriented, and spoil you. But do you meet your own requirements? If not, it's time for a little reevaluation.

A relationship should be viewed as a partnership, not a sponsorship. You should not be looking for someone to take care of you. One of the best feelings to have is a sense of accomplishment. Your goal should not be to be sponsored by someone. If things don't work out as planned, where does that leave you financially? There will be times where you may need help. And that's okay. What's not okay is to solely depend on the funds of another.

We no longer reside in the olden days, where all women can stay home and take care of the house and kids. And this is no diss to those hard-working fellas providing for their families and loved ones. But, yes, we women are out there working hard at our jobs, studying even harder for school, building legacies, and trying to take care of the home and children. Some of us cannot do the simple things in life because we are so busy trying to keep our heads above water. We are trying to set examples for our offspring, while also attempting to maintain a relationship. If there is no balance, that relationship will lose its spontaneity and it will slowly fade away. We must learn to juggle both. Not everything will work for everyone. It's trial and error.

One day, my daughter and I were lying around watching television. She turned to me and said, "Ma?"

I looked at her.

She said, "It doesn't make you feel some type of way that you and Kevin don't spend much time together? Both of y'all work during the day, and then y'all come home. He goes downstairs to edit work on the computer and you're up here in the room. If he isn't editing, then he's at the gym."

While she had a very valid point, I explained to her that our routine is what works for us. Sometimes we may get a bit off track. But otherwise, we had a routine and we stuck with it, still to this day.

Kevin and I came up with a systematic way of doing things. We pulled out the dry-erase calendar board, marker, and miniature-sized post-its. Filling in the board, we began to stick post-it notes of our daily "to-do's" on days of the week, accordingly. For example, on Mondays, Wednesdays, and Fridays, Kevin would work out, then come home and edit for his production company. Tuesdays and Thursdays would be my

days to exercise and write. I would even join him at the gym on days
Jasmine babysat our son, her little brother, Joey. Of course, during
those times, we were working a nine-to-five job, taking care of the kids,
and maintaining the household. On weekends, we would relax and enjoy
each other's company. Sometimes, we'd deviate from the "plan," but we
also understood that there were goals needing to be met. So, we
continued in forward motion.

Again, some things will not work for you. You and your mate must
sit down and devise a plan. More importantly, you have to stick to it. At
first, it may seem a bit redundant, but once you become acclimated to
your schedule, it becomes second nature to you.

Maybe you are someone who was in a relationship, and you did all
of the aforementioned. But, for whatever reason, your partner was not on
the same track as you. Respect yourself enough to know when to let go.
In life, there are some people you are going to have to lose in order to find
yourself. But understand that everyone you lose is not a loss. Love is a
non-guaranteed commitment. More often than not, people stay in failed
relationships for all the wrong reasons. You do not feel like starting over
again. You don't want to look like a failure to the outside world. You
have gotten comfortable with your mate. Perhaps, you are waiting for a
miracle to happen. Whatever the case, there is no reason to hold
yourself back for a person who clearly does not want to comply with the
demands associated with a relationship. Do not settle. You should not

continue to give someone all of what you have if they cannot appreciate half of what you've given. Knowing you deserve better is just half the battle.

Do not spend hours on end wondering why you were wronged. Worry about loving yourself instead of pondering over the thought of others loving you. You will have people in your life telling you to get over it. Personally, I dislike those "get over it" type of people. You have the right to heal at your own pace. You are allowed to take your time. Ignore those who rush you because they do not understand the magnitude of your pain. It is easy for people to tell you to get over it until they have to be the ones to get over it.

Refrain from entering a new relationship until you have healed from your failed one. Carrying broken pieces of you into a new partnership is a sure-fire way of ending it before it starts.

Once you are ready to enter a new relationship, be cognizant of the fact that not everyone is the same. It is imperative to understand that your new mate is not your old mate. Do not make anyone else suffer for your ex's mistakes. Not only is it unfair. It is creating a barrier between the two of you, unbeknownst to your lover.

When it comes to healing, there is no sense of urgency. Be wise in your decision-making. Just because you want someone does not mean that person deserves to have you. Be patient, but not stagnant. Remain hopeful, but not naïve. It is perfectly fine to allow yourself time to pick up the pieces and restore your faith in the possibility of a successful relationship. After all, love isn't magical. It takes work.

II.

A relationship with your mate is not the only type of relationship you should concern yourself with. When I became a mother, I did not completely know what to expect. I understood the many things motherhood consisted of. I watched lots of children grow up in good and not-so-good environments. I knew good parenting from bad parenting. What I didn't expect was just how selfless I would become. I knew that I would have to protect my children. What I did not anticipate was my complete, unhesitant willingness to lay my life on the line for them. If you are anything like myself, then your children are your world. Whether you have one child or many, your love for them is unconditional. You just want the best for them. You want a great relationship.

Having a relationship, let alone a good one, with your children takes one hundred percent dedication. It is very realistic for us to expect our children to respect us. Along with that has to come much respect from us as well. If we are trying to raise kings and queens, then we must behave ourselves as such.

As with many things, wanting a great outcome on a relationship with your children starts with how you initiate it. From day one, your main focus should be to always hold your kids in high regard. Do not assume that because you have a baby who is not speaking or walking, that he or she is not observing your every move. Children are sponges; they absorb everything they see and hear. If you have random partners around your child, you have already begun to plant a negative seed. Children need to be shown consistency. While casually dating, if the person your children see is not their parent, then they do not need to see that person. While it is perfectly fine to date, your children should not be seeing these potentials. They should be completely oblivious of the fact that you aren't in a committed relationship. Keep your private life just that, private.

When I first met up with Kevin, it was nowhere near my home. Being a single mother, I kept safety at the top of my list. A year into our relationship, I still did not introduce him to my children. Although I enjoyed our time spent, despite the ups and downs, I still was not sure if he was "the one."

After about two years, I slowly brought up his name through casual conversation with my kids. They actually did not believe he existed. They thought I was lying, which I found to be comforting and hilarious at the same time. My oldest brother, Darryl, even had a nickname for Kevin...secret lover. To me, their doubt of his existence was reassuring to me. It meant that I did what I sought out to do, not let my private life intertwine with the lives of my children and me.

After two and a half years, I finally introduced them. They meshed well and still do. Because I respected my children enough not to bring anyone else into our circle without their approval, they were able to develop their own unique bonds with Kevin, as opposed to feeling forced to bond due to my selfishness.

While two and a half years was quite a lengthy amount of time to wait to introduce my children to Kevin, it worked for me. Again, I needed my kids to understand that they were my main priorities, and nothing or no one came before them. You may not need to wait that long. However, you must take time to get to know your partner before bringing your children into the mix.

If you are on the dating scene, you must find a way to balance your life with your prospective partner and your life with your children. They need to be certain that they are your first priority and nothing will interfere with that. Because you believe you are in love, do not force your children to feel the same. Let them develop their own thoughts and feelings toward your mate. Doing anything else will cause a rift between you and them, thus affecting your relationship negatively.

If you are in a relationship with the parent of your child/children, it is vital that you two maintain a healthy relationship, particularly for the sake of the kids. Raising them in a warm, trusting, stable environment, where you two display the utmost respect for one another, instills value in your children, which is indicative of being a successful individual. It would be absurd to think that disagreements will not happen. Nonetheless, it would be thoughtless for you two to parade these disparities in front of your children. If you and your mate begin to quarrel, excuse yourself into the bedroom. Respect your children's feelings. At that particular moment, you may hate your mate's guts. However, that mate is still your children's parent, and their love for that parent is unconditional. Do not talk down about the other parent to your children. You will unknowingly force your offspring to associate one parent as the good parent, while labeling the other parent as bad. You will also inadvertently compel your children into subconsciously labeling one parent as their favorite. Your dysfunctional relationship, if any, has absolutely nothing to do with the relationship between that other parent and your children. Give them the choice to decide what is and what is not acceptable to them.

Being realistic, lots of people are no longer in a relationship with the parent of their children. Although the situation is different, one thing remains the same. You must still respect one another for the sake of the kids. They do not need to be subjected to their parents' constant bickering and disrespect for one another. Your differences must be set to the side in order to maintain healthy relationships amongst everyone.

Because you are jealous or despise your ex's new mate, you should not be altering your children's relationship with the opposite parent. And because you are with a new mate, your children's relationship with their other parent should not dwindle because you want to keep your new "boo" happy. A child needs both parents. A new partner who does not support or promote a relationship between you and your children is not worth having. If you are with someone who demands more of your time than you give your offspring, it is time to seek the single life until someone more understanding comes along.

Being the mother of two headstrong kids, I have learned to respect their boundaries, while still making my role as their mother understood. It took many restless nights and long days for me to come to terms with the fact that my children aren't babies anymore and that they need their space. I knew my daughter was at the age where she would begin to like boys. I was aware that my son was approaching the stages of becoming sexually active. Instead of being closed-minded to the thoughts and curiosities of my teens, I decided to approach them, both in a different manner.

With my son, I understood that, although we had a great relationship, I could not take the place of his absentee father. There were those father/son conversations and moments he never got to have. But I was hell bent on creating an everlasting bond between the two of us. And I was not about to let his pubescent years cause a wedge between us. Everything, from his voice to his demeanor, was changing. Therefore, I began to study these small changes and conformed to them, accordingly.

When I noticed that he desired some alone time, I let him be. Whenever he wanted to talk, I was at his disposal. Once he realized I respected his space, he started to let me into his world more and more. During those moments, I was able to ask the tough questions a parent needs to know. He opened up to me, which allowed me to provide the proper guidance on the matters. I don't profess to know every single thing about my son. However, because he let me in as much as he did, I was able to build a bond with him to where he realizes he can talk to me about anything, if he so desires. Although he's off into the world and making a name for himself in the Air Force, he knows I'm only a FaceTime or a call away.

With my daughter, it was a bit more difficult. Being a teenage girl, she felt compelled to look a certain way. Her hormones were making her extremely moody. She would sometimes shut down, even closing herself in her room. Because she has always been a heavy talker during her prepubescent years, it was easy for me to spot when something was wrong. Not wanting to scare her off, I decided that I had to create an environment in which she was not afraid to talk to me.

Unlike my son being given his space, I had to invade hers a little. When I would notice her being locked away in her room, I would ask for "permission" to come in. I would strike up minor conversations with her, asking her about her day, what was going on with her and her friends, inquire about what she was watching on TV, and whatever else would come to mind. I developed a pattern of constant conversation with her. I would then find times for us to bond outside the home, taking her with me to the store, or even going to get manicures. Once she was aware I was interested in things other than her teenage issues, it was then that she decided to slowly open up to me. She did not feel like I was just being nosey, but more so that I had an interest in her everyday living.

One day, I asked her to accompany me to a breakfast restaurant. She obliged. Once we arrived and were seated, she and I talked about what we should do for the rest of the day. After twenty minutes or so, I elected to have a heart-to-heart with her. I knew that, although there were things she wanted to discuss, she was unsure if she should.

So I asked her, "Jasmine, do you ever think about having a boyfriend?"

Once I said that, she looked at me and smiled. And for the remainder of our breakfast date, I could not get her to be quiet. She began to talk about everything: boys, fake friends, her body image, and even her future aspirations. I was happy. From that point on, I made myself completely accessible to her. I did so because I knew that not being there could be detrimental to our relationship. We still bump heads, but she knows that I am here for her, always.

Your children deserve your love and respect. They need proper guidance from you. It should be your mission to raise your children to be a better version of yourself. But you must understand that this will not happen if you are not laying the foundation. Keep in mind that everything you do, your kids can be affected by.

Learn your children. Understand what upsets them, hurts them, and makes them happy. Know their favorite foods, colors, and sports. The more you know about your children, the better equipped you are to raise and assist them. Invest in their dreams. Build a plan for their futures and do not wait until the last minute. Make time for them. Create unforgettable memories.

III.

Some of us were not blessed to have both parents in our lives. And, if they were there, maybe they weren't the best at being a parent.

As mentioned earlier, my mother and father separated when I was eleven years old. When they parted, I was lost. My mental and emotional state was damaged. How would I live life with my dad not being around? Who was going to tuck me in at night or sneak me my midnight snack? It was a difficult time in my life. The only male I could truly depend on, during that time, was my older brother Darryl. But still, he wasn't our father.

As time progressed, my relationship with my dad diminished. We barely spoke to one another. When we did speak, much time would pass before we spoke again. I did not see my father. I was growing up and he was not around. I was sad because he missed some of the most significant times of my life. When my grandmother passed away from cancer, he was not there. A year later, I graduated from eighth grade. He was not there. When my favorite aunt died two years after, from cancer, he was not there. I went to prom and graduated high school. He still was not there. I grew resentful because I could not understand what I did to deserve that. He was distant, in what felt to be every aspect of my life. All I had was my mother, older brother, and now my younger brother, Vonte.

As time passed, my mother worked two jobs at a time, trying to provide for the three of us, as my little brother's father was absent in his life as well. She struggled, but she always did what she had to do to keep food in our bellies and a roof over our heads. She was tenacious, and I admired her. Everyone did. She was, and still is, a jack-of-all-trades. She did not understand the magnitude of my respect for her.

It was not until my early adult years that I had begun to reestablish a consistent relationship with my father. Yes, we spoke here and there throughout the years. However, it was not enough for me to be able to say that my dad knew what type of individual I had grown to become. We had to learn each other all over again, in a sense. He apologized, and I forgave him for not being there. And even though I was still hurting, I knew that I had to let go of the past if I wanted to move forward. I love my father...always have and always will. But I just had to accept what things once were and move forward, for my own sanity.

One of the many reasons I tried to stay in contact with my father was because I would be devastated if he expired and I was not a part of his life. Well, in February of 2017, that almost happened. My dad had numerous strokes and heart attacks. He was in the hospital for what seemed like an eternity. I was there every step of the way. I needed to be. Again, he was not a continuous force in my life. But the minute I decided to forgive, I no longer let the fact that he was absent have any bearing on our newfound relationship.

Not only did my father and I mend our once broken relationship and lack of communication, I was able to gain a plethora of siblings from it all. During these years, I was able to stay in contact with my four sisters (Annette, Kim, Nakia, and Ashley) and two brothers (Ricardo and Justin). Yes, my father had quite a few children. And although we are all in a total of three different states, we remain in contact with one another.

My first encounter with love was the love given to me by my parents. This is the same for you as well. How we are loved by our parents/guardians can determine how we view love and give it to others. If you received unconditional love during your childhood, then it is not far-fetched to believe that you will pass that love on to others just as you acquired it. However, if you had a parent who did not express their love for you, who put work before family, who spent more time disciplining you rather than getting to know you, or who put others before you, then you may feel unloved or unimportant. Feeling that way will affect you negatively, which will also spill over into your adult life as well. You must find a way to accept what was and move forward. Tell your parents you are forgiving them so that you can move on. Your forgiveness does not have to be as important to them as it is for your own levelheadedness.

You must understand that your parents are human, too. While they may not have been the best at it, you have to learn to let go of anything weighing you down. It does not mean you are okay with the mistakes made, but that you choose to overcome it for your own well-being. You have a life worth living. So, move forward and learn to live it. You owe it to yourself to continue being the best version of yourself possible.

IV.

Friendships are another form of relationships we come across in our lives. It is nothing like having the type of people you can count on, no matter what. When you are having bad times, you count on your friends. You got the job you have been praying for. You call on your friends to share the great news. Bad break-up? Your friends become your therapy. When you are bored, you reach out to your friends to see what you all can get into.

Whether you realize it or not, friendship is an important part of our daily living. We may rely on our parents, siblings, cousins, and even our lovers to get us through a situation or give us advice. But sometimes, we just need to share our uncertainties and indiscretions with our friends.

My definition of a friend is someone I can confide in. It is someone I have a strong bond with, who supports me, who I trust wholeheartedly, who pushes me to be a better person, and who share the same values as I do. We can agree to disagree. We balance one another. We can go days or weeks without talking. And when we do, our vibe has not changed.

As simple as it may seem, true friendships are hard to come by. Too many people throw the "friend" word around without understanding all that it entails. Some do not perceive what it takes to be a friend, while others are just incapable of being one.

As young children, it is common to view just about every child you have an interaction with as your friend. Your classmates are your friends, as well as the children who live on the same block as you. When you get older, you become more aware of what a genuine friendship should look and feel like. You have a better understanding of what a true friend is. Nevertheless, you still make mistakes when picking them.

As you have heard before, some people are meant to be in your life for a reason, while others for a season. Not everyone you come across will be there forever, even the ones you thought you could not live without. Instances will arise, where you will find yourself by yourself. You are counting on your best friend to come and rescue you from the temporary pain you are having, but that best friend of yours is nowhere to be found. What happened?

When choosing friends, be mindful that you are the company you keep. You and your friends should be on one accord. Choosing friends is similar to picking fruits and vegetables. When you go to the grocery store, do you just grab the first piece of fruit or vegetable you see? Or do you examine it, look at its texture and shape, feel for its ripeness, smell it, and then choose one, based off of what best suits you?

The same method you use when picking fruits and vegetables should be the same when picking friends. When you meet someone, you two should not become friends instantly. Study the characteristics of and get to know this person. Is he or she conducive to your everyday living? Goal oriented? Intelligent? Driven? What common interests do you share? These are some of the things you should be asking yourself when choosing friends. The more you know about people, the easier it is to decipher whether or not they are a good fit for you.

A friend should inspire you to reach your goals, motivate you to do better and be a better person than you were yesterday, and help you keep your priorities intact. Although your friend will still see and do things differently than you, this should not hurt your bond with one another. You and your friend should also, unequivocally, agree that loyalty is significant in your roles to one another.

The older I became, the more I realized what friendship was about. I learned that not everyone I considered to be a friend actually was. It was during my darkest hours when I grasped the reality of who my friends really were. I saw that many who claimed to be loyal was, in fact, quite the opposite. I could not pinpoint where the disconnect had come from. But in my heart, I knew it was time to let it go. These friends of mine appeared to be friends with anyone and everyone. They were people pleasers. It was then that I understood Aristotle's famous quote, "A friend to all is a friend to none."

Loyalty is essential to an everlasting friendship. It can make it or break it. At least once in your life, you will learn that someone close to you has not been loyal. Continuing a friendship with someone who does not possess the ability to be loyal is unquestionably unhealthy. It's like putting a band-aid on a scar. You do it for temporary healing, but underneath that band-aid, the scar remains. The same goes for an unhealthy friendship. If your friend has proven to be disloyal or disrespectful to the relationship you two share, no invisible band-aid will ever fix it. If your friend has wronged you, you must find it in your heart to forgive, for your own peace of mind. If the cycle of deceit continues, the strings need to be cut. Will it be easy? No. Doable? Absolutely. Patience is a virtue.

Every now and then, you may find yourself trying to salvage that one friendship you thought would never end. If you have done all you can, yet the other party isn't willing, take it as a sign. Again, not everyone who enters your life is meant to stay. They could be lessons along the way. Accept the fact that you two no longer have ties, cherish the good times, bury the hatchet, and move forward.

In life, you will realize that there is a purpose for everyone you meet. Some are there to test you. Some will use you. Some will teach you. Some will bring out the best in you. Do not waste time fighting for something that is not meant to be. It may hurt, but the decision to move forward is right. What seems like the right thing to do could also be the hardest thing you have ever done in your life. The only people you need in your life are the ones who willingly need you in theirs. Know where you stand with people. You are only going to be as happy as you allow yourself be. Once more, forgive and proceed ahead.

Forgiving is definitely not for the other person. It is for you. You must do so in order to move on, even if it means forgiving those who never even apologized. That is true character. Once you pardon anyone who has wronged you, you exonerate yourself from a life of unnecessary

stress and burden.

Chapter Four

Be Your Own Company

I. Acquire Some Me Time

II. Pamper Yourself

I.

This chapter won't be long, so let's just cut to the chase. While it is great to have friends around to support you, you need to be okay with being your own company. You have to be able to be at peace with knowing that, at any given moment, it's you against the world.

As sad as reality is, we must face the fact that our friends and family are human, which means they are prone to making mistakes and upsetting us. Although it shouldn't alter your relationships, it is still healthy to take a step back and be perfectly fine with providing yourself some much needed me time.

Me time is not a selfish act. In fact, it is essential to everyday living and functioning. No matter how busy your work week is, there is always a way to make time for yourself. Of the 1,440 minutes in a day, seven days in a week, there are no excuses as to why you cannot achieve at least an hour or two a week of some me time. You do not have supernatural powers. You need time to readjust and refocus in order to provide your loved ones with the best refueled version of yourself.

As a mom, I once found this hard to accomplish. My guilt would kick in, having me feeling like I could be doing something more productive with my time for others more so than for myself. Wrong! I had to realize that if I am not the best version of myself, how could I expect my kids to be the best version of themselves? It's not possible.

Understanding the importance of me time will help you gain insight as to why it is much needed. Me time allows you to capture better insight and clarity, thus improving your focus and concentration.

I'm sure there are times when your thoughts are all over the place. And before you can finish your previous thought, you are already formulating a new one. This plays into your mental health. Allow yourself some time for a soothing technique such as yoga, meditation, or even rest. Sometimes, focusing on nothing is the best type of mental stimulation one could ever acquire. We don't always have to be in constant thought. Clear your mind in order to allow new thoughts and ideas to enter it. I recently started meditation, and so far, it's the best thing since sliced bread!

Me time is significant when it comes to being of service to others. I have a nonprofit organization where we feed and clothe the underprivileged throughout the year. If I am not taking time to care for myself, to look presentable, and to be mentally strong, how can I anticipate those less fortunate than myself to acquire good vibes from me if I'm unable to give them off? When people depend on you, you need to make sure you are in a state where you can offer the type of assistance they need. The underprivileged don't need to see me looking frazzled, discombobulated, and like I haven't slept in days. They need to see me looking rejuvenated and ready to lend a helping hand. In order for me successfully help them, I don't need to just look or act the part. I need to be the part! I need to show up, looking and sounding my best because those people are depending on me to brighten their day, even if it is just for five minutes.

Going back to the health aspect of it, me time is not only significant for mental health, but it's much needed to maintain your health, overall. Let's face it. Our bodies go through a lot. Sleepless nights and early days are times we have all encountered. Dang it! You forgot to wash that last load of clothes. Oops, no time because little Katie has to be to dance practice in thirty minutes. So, you disregard the fact that you haven't slept in what seems like an eternity, you grab that coffee, and you head out to handle your business. After a while, you may feel fine. But guess what doesn't? Your body.

You must realize that you only get one temple. Once you run your body to the ground, you don't get to go pick out another one at the store up the street. And before long, your body will slowly begin to shut down on you. Like the saying goes, "If you don't take care of your health today, you will be forced to take care of your illness tomorrow." Never let it get to that point. Invest time in yourself.

Me time means learning to say "no" to people. Sure, you promised your friend that you guys could go grab a cocktail on your day off. Yes, you told your sister you would do her hair when you got off work. Okay, you gave your homeboy your word that you two can catch Sunday night football together. But if you're delegating your time to everyone else, where's your time for you? Declining someone's offer doesn't make you a bad person, nor does it make you unreliable. It simply means that you have decided to put life on hold for a slight second in order to better yourself. Any true friend or family member will understand that.

Last, but certainly not least, me time is vital when it comes to overall happiness. Imagine how much happier you could be if you just steal a few moments to care for yourself, love on yourself, and spoil yourself. Never forget that you are just as important as the people that depend on you. Obligations and responsibilities will always be around, until we exit this lifetime. But that does not mean to disregard yourself in the process. Again, be okay with being your own company. You'd be surprised how much you can learn about yourself.

II.

Now that you know how vital me time is, let's chat about ways to make sure it happens.

As mentioned before, you must set aside some me time. This is not up for debate. It is imperative that you seek a method that can help to ease your stress and clear your mind. Once more, yoga, meditation, and plain ol' rest will do the trick. Yoga and meditation go hand in hand. While yoga helps improve flexibility, balance, and strength, meditation can assist in the strengthening of your immune system, as well as aid in relieving stress and lowering blood pressure.

When I started meditating, it was hard for me to stay focused. This may come easy for some, and challenging for others. Your main objective is to think of nothing. The whole point is to clear your mind. While there are different meditation techniques, I am fond of two: mindfulness meditation and breath awareness meditation.

Although they are similar, mindfulness meditation is about being aware and present in your moment. Your only job is to sit or lie there, clear your mind, and focus on nothing. Thoughts will pop into your head, but the key to mindfulness meditation is to relieve yourself of that thought and get back to a clear head.

Breath awareness meditation focuses solely on your breathing. Simple enough, right? Focusing on how your lungs expand, the rise and fall of your chest, and how slowly and deeply you breathe are all parts of this meditation. As boring as it may sound, the effects are nothing short of amazing, once done correctly.

Nothing screams relaxing like a massage. There are many to choose from: Swedish, hot stone, deep tissue, and aromatherapy, just to name a few. Take time to find the nearest spa to you, and invest a little money into a nice pampering session. Then head out and get yourself a manicure and pedicure. Men, this goes for you as well! There is nothing feminine about providing yourself a pampering session.

Something as simple as eating your lunch in the park instead of with your coworkers can help put you in a calm state of mind.

One that we may find the most challenging of all is to disconnect from the world; silence your cellphone, unplug your radio, power off your television. Leave social media alone and savor your solitude.

When planning me time, you absolutely have to stand your ground and make sure it happens...no excuses. If it means putting off dinner for thirty minutes, then do so. Remember, you are just as important as anyone else.

While enjoying your me time, be sure to stay blissful. Treat yourself well, and it will rub off into other aspects of your daily living. Understand that self-care is not optional. Set the tone for how others view and treat you. Ineluctably, some little human being watches you, at one point or another. It may be your child, niece, nephew, or cousin. No matter who it is, be sure to be a positive, healthy force in their lives. Me time will help you accomplish just that.

Chapter Five

Cyberworld

I. "Meme" What You Say

II. Social Media Courting

III. Relationships on Social

Media

I.

Let's face it. Nowadays, people will talk the talk, but dare not walk the walk. These are the times where, instead of communicating like mature adults, people search for the best meme to suit their momentary feelings of rejection, betrayal, or pure hatred. Then, they post them in the form of a subliminal message, in hopes that their target receives it. Welcome to the cyberworld.

We live in a world driven by social media. Face to face communication is a thing of the past...for some people. It's no longer about human interaction. It's about taking the time to search Google for the most suitable meme, spitefully posting it, and waiting for your enemy, for better lack of words, to respond. Maybe it's not an enemy. Maybe it's someone you've had a quarrel with. Maybe it's someone who secretly envies you. Maybe it's someone who despises you. Maybe it's someone who just can't stand to see you happy. Whatever the case, the fix to the problem is not to address it like a mature person, but to publicly rant about it without you ever knowing there was a problem to begin with. And by the time you do know, the situation has already been blown out of proportion, probably beyond genuine repair, all because of a cowardly act of social media bashing.

Social media, primarily Facebook, Instagram, and Twitter, has given people platforms to be someone they're not, to do things in the cyberworld that they wouldn't dream of in real life. This, by far, is the most disheartening act one could display. Let us just focus on Facebook right now, for the sake of argument.

I mean, let's just be honest. The dependence some have on social media, for validation purposes, is at an all-time high. In the real world, you cannot hide who you truly are, or what you really possess. But, as for Facebook, there's no such thing as "the proof is in the pudding." You can be whoever you want to be, have anything you want to have, and say anything against another person because there is little to no accountability being held. Moreover, most of the people presenting this public facade know they will never see many of their Facebook friends in real life.

Believing in yourself and your capabilities is no longer confirmed through your own beliefs, but from the red hearts and comments of others. It is now a matter of how many likes are received and how many positive remarks are given. Facebook is no longer a place to go for entertainment; it is now a necessity, for many, in order to function. People envy others, not even knowing if what they are envying is in fact legit. Someone gets less likes, and suddenly the person who receives more feels superior. Karen has five thousand friends. So, now she feels significant. It doesn't even matter that most of those five thousand friends are people she doesn't even know. It just matters that they are her "friends." Robert woke up to forty-two friend requests because of his publicly posted picture of his 2019 Lexus ES, so his social status has gone up. There's only one thing. That Lexus isn't his, but no one knows because he doesn't have to prove it. As long as one's ego is being fed, they are content. As long as the likes keep coming, everything is perfectly fine.

Going back to social media bashing, although memes are quite entertaining, they are now being used to replace verbal communication. They have taken over the internet. Instead of memes being used as something to make others laugh, they are used to offend them. If you aren't careful, you will get swept into the meme feud as well. You will find yourself going back and forth with someone, in an attempt to assassinate their character, just as they did you. I can honestly say I did it for a couple of months. I allowed the injustices of memes to get to me. Not channeling my frustration, I decided to fire back. It was all fun and games until I realized that I gained absolutely nothing from it. I had to do a reality check. I had to be real enough with myself to say, "Kita, what the hell are you doing? You know who you are and what you stand for!" Once I decided that no number of offensive memes could replace what my verbal skills could acquire in real life, I let the "beef" go.

Anytime your validation comes from social media, you are in a whirl of trouble. If you need strangers to tell you that you're beautiful, you lack self-confidence. If you rely on people you barely know or rarely communicate with to boost your ego, you are already two steps behind. Seek help! No one's social status should be tied up into the cyberworld.

Communication is extremely vital in any aspect of life. Personally, I think people should do social media detoxes. Put yourself back into the real world. Understand that, while you control your Facebook account, you cannot control what happens if and when you are confronted face to face. Learn that to be angry is okay, but to spitefully bash someone is not the way to go.

Touching on why people feel the need to be validated on social media, it all boils down to one thing... lack of self-worth. Changing who you are for likes only means that you are not actually being liked for who you truly are. Any number of likes, whether high or low, does not define you. A high number does not mean you are the shit. A low number does not mean you are complete shit. It means nothing. What matters is your opinion of yourself. Your self-based opinion should be the only thing that can make or break you. Be you, whoever you are! Just because Keisha gets hundreds of likes for showing her cleavage in every other picture does not mean you should go showing yours. If Nate gets likes because he flashes his money on a daily basis, you shouldn't go parading yours.

If you've never heard of the Netflix series titled, "You," I highly suggest checking it out. It's centered around a young lady who creates this façade online of having such a wonderful, happy life. But, in reality, her life is in shambles, she's robbing Peter to pay Paul, her boyfriend is far from supportive, she's trying to keep up with the Joneses, and her friends are about as fake as they come. This is much like a lot of people on social media. They post this picture-perfect life, all for likes and attention, yet they sit at home miserable, comparing themselves to the next person.

Understand that not everyone will like you, and be okay with that. Personally, I could care less if tons of people like me. My circle is so small, yet full of genuine, loyal, down to Earth people. They get me, I get them, and we have mutual understandings. I do not believe in keeping a crowd of people around me. Follow the crowd, and you lose yourself. Stand alone, and you find yourself. You should be focused less on your fake social media status, and more on your self-worth. Besides, half the people giving you false Facebook praises will be nowhere to be found when you find yourself in a bind, needing someone to lean on.

Stop worrying about pleasing people. Stop tying your value up into social media. Stop thinking that those praising you have your best interests at heart. Stop comparing your pictures to others. Stop getting happy when you receive another red heart. Stop lurking. Stop trolling. Stop competing. Just stop! You are you, and they are them. Walk your path and let them walk theirs. Do what's best for you and never mind the rest.

We are all different. Although we may share some of the same views, we are still divergent by nature. Learn to accept who you are and live with it. If you are changing who you are, do it for you! If those in your life, or on your social media pages, cannot accept who you truly are, then delete them. If you don't like what someone is saying on their page, block them. If the sight of someone makes your skin crawl, unfriend them. If you sense even a wee bit of hate, do away with the hater. It's all about protecting your space.

In essence, be real with yourself. Be true to yourself. Love who you are. Accept the fact that you are beautifully flawed. And most importantly, MEME what you say and say what you MEME!

II.

Remember the good ol' days when you attended safe house parties? Remember how that old radio in the basement would play one of the best slow jams, like Keith Sweat's "Right and a Wrong Way," and a guy would ask you to dance? Then, you two would dance close enough to pick up on that "I got a crush on you" vibe, but far enough as to where you could still look down and see space between your pants zipper and his because your auntie was in the corner watching y'all? What about when you gave or received that note which read "I like you. Do you like me? Check "yes or no"?" Recollect the times where guys didn't see how big of a butt you had, because that Sunday school dress your mother used to put on you, the one with the pleats all around it, did not show your backside. Or what about the slips your mother or grandmother used to throw on you that dare not show your panty line? How about the days when a guy came to pick you up for a date, and he actually got out of his car, rang the doorbell, and spoke to your parents instead of pulling up, blowing his horn and texting you saying, "I'm outside?"

Those were the good, innocent days. Those were the days where people actually got to know one another. There was no social media. There were no cell phones... just pure, unadulterated face to face connections. There was no texting. You spoke verbally or wrote notes. You picked up that rotary phone, spun that dial around, and waited for the person on the receiving end to answer. If you were on the phone too long, your parents or siblings would pick up the phone from another part of the house and tell you that your time is up. Ahhh...those were the days!

Now, it seems as if chivalry is dead. Lots of men and women have decided that the best way to capture a person's heart and attention is through Facebook messenger, or Instagram DM. What? Really? Don't get me wrong. I'm all for online connections. I see nothing wrong with it.

71

But to replace face to face encounters with instant messaging is completely absurd.

Social media has made it easy for people to be someone other than who they really are. Catfishing is at an all-time high. You're so busy chatting it up in messenger, getting to know the person whose profile picture you fell in lust with, that when you two finally meet, you're absolutely appalled. Why? Because the person on that profile picture, the person who posted so much about their beach body, the person who claimed to have several successful businesses is not the person standing in front of you. The person standing in front of you cannot put on a filter. The person standing in front of you cannot photoshop their body. The person standing in front of you cannot provide proof of those successful businesses they constantly posted about.

Social media courting is very misleading. Again, I'm all for meeting someone via Facebook, Instagram, and dating apps. However, there comes a time where the DM's need to stop, the messaging needs to cease, and the two potentials need to man up and come face to face.

When I open up a message from an unknown guy, and the first thing he tells me about is how beautiful he thinks my body is, I hit that "delete" button. When I open a DM and the first thing I read about is how bad a guy wants to taste my kitty, I block him. I don't block him only because I'm in a committed relationship. I block him because he has shown to me that he lacks the proper communication skills to be

72

able to reach my level of intellect. I am not turned on by dick pics in my messenger, or by the fact that you want to lick me from my head to toe. Save it. I'm good, love. Any woman, in her right mind, should not be doing happy flips when she receives such repulsive messages.

The same goes for a guy. Any self-respecting man will not relish the thought of being with a woman who just sent him a picture of her half naked body. A true gentleman will not get excited about receiving a message from a woman who initially shows interest in material possessions.

Being completely factual, about one in five relationships begin online. But, again, people are lying on these online dating apps and social media profiles. One of the biggest lies being told by women pertains to their physical characteristics; for men, it's their financial status.

Fellas, imagine getting handsome, looking like you just stepped out of GQ magazine, to go have a drink with the lady you met on Facebook, only to see someone standing in front of you that you don't even recognize. Ladies, picture that man you met in your DM rolling up to come chill with you, only to realize that he does not have that 2019 Lexus he constantly posts about, but that he was dropped off by Uber.

All of this may sound superficial, but the truth of the matter is that it is happening. What may have initially attracted you to someone can

73

be the very reason the fling doesn't work out because what you saw is not what you got.

Once again, online dating apps and social media hook ups are not a taboo subject. However, be mindful of the fact that you may be setting yourself up for failure. Drop the phones, unplug the computers, disconnect from Wi-Fi, and go out into the real world. Hit the dance floor again. Guys, instead of sending rose emojis, hand deliver them. Ladies, instead of sending "I love you" gifs, tell him face to face. Chivalry and grace do not have to be a thing of the past. Bring it back.

III.

Depending on the individuals, social media can do more harm to a relationship than good. It is no longer an intimate "you and me" type of situation. It's more of an "us versus them" state of mind.

Back in the day, relationships had privacy and spontaneity. When there were misunderstandings, two people could choose to talk it out or walk away without somehow still be connected to their ex. In today's society, people don't even understand the importance of keeping your love life to yourself. Sometimes, I feel like I know more about people's relationships than they do, simply because they post anything and everything about it on social media. I can tell if Kylie and Joe are having an issue because Kylie always posts subliminal messages whenever she is feeling some type of way. It's easy for me to know when Don and Theresa go on private getaways because that private moment was publicly posted.

Relationships have lost its meaning along the way, all because some people feel the need to tell the world everything about it. But here lies the problem; when you constantly let people in on every detail of your relationship, you've already rid yourself of secrecy and intimacy, thus granting permission for others to dive in and scrutinize. Please know and understand that when you post about how your partner has pissed you off, you're leaving room for someone else to swoop in to make your partner happy in ways they feel you cannot.

There are so many reasons you should not be posting every moment of your relationship on social media. For one, it can cause you to jump to conclusions and make rash decisions.

Let's say your boyfriend told you he was going out with the guys, yet a female makes a comment on his page about how nice it was to see him on that same night he was out. Your mind is going to race like never before. "Oh, so he lied to me? He didn't tell me females would be with him and the guys!" Not once did you stop to think maybe that female was someone who knows his sister, or that they could've gone to grammar school together. Although nothing he did was deceitful, you immediately conjured up the thought that he was out doing something other than what he told you he was doing.

I've seen it numerous times where women feel like their partner is trying to hide them or keep them a secret because their face isn't plastered all over their partner's page. How much your man or woman posts you does not equal how much they care about and love you. Sure, you see how your best friend's man professes his love for her on his page almost every other day. That does not mean that your man doesn't love you. Stop looking for false reassurances on social media. Maybe your man is not into wanting other men to gawk at his woman. Maybe your man is just a private man who gets that not everyone needs to know his business. Maybe your woman knows how other women can be and she doesn't want to risk having other women hitting you up in messenger. Women can be very messy. Besides, not every wonderfully posted relationship you see is wonderful. It's called "fronting."

Special moments become less genuine when you continuously share them for the world to see. Your partner decided to surprise you with a private weekend getaway...just the two of you. But, somehow, you managed to turn that "two of you" into a social media affair because you chose to post every special moment of it. "We are boarding the plane guys!" "Look at this beautiful hotel room!" "Headed to the beach with my man!" "He just bought me this Louis Vuitton purse!" "Having wine on the balcony!" "Look at how my dress is hugging my body!" "He loves me!" Enough already! What he would probably love is if you put your damn phone down and be more into him than you are social media.

Here's one. You and your mate have decided to go your separate ways. Instead of moving on, you decide to watch his or her every move via social media. There was none of this back in the day. Once the relationship was over, you had minimal access to your ex, unless you were stalking or being stalked! Now, you can't even properly close the door to your past because you're too busy trolling your ex's page trying to see what they're up to and with whom. Let it go. You guys are exes for a reason.

I am not saying that it's not okay to post a picture of your mate, or to say something genuine to your sweetheart on social media. I'm simply trying to convey to you that you should keep your love life's most precious moments between you and your partner. I would be lying if I said I didn't post pictures of me and my boyfriend. However, the best moments of our relationship don't make it to social media. When we are disputing, the world never knows because I refuse to subject our relationship to scrutiny. My relationship isn't your business and yours isn't mine. Learn to keep that intimacy amongst you two. Treat your relationship like you do your pin number to your bank card, confidential.

Chapter Six

Taking Control

I. Toxicity

II. Do You!

I.

During your lifetime, you will come across people who judge and criticize many things you do. They take no responsibility for their actions, are manipulative, inconsistent, untrustworthy, and always play the victim. These people are constantly putting you in positions to defend yourself. Yet, you find yourself putting up with it because of your ties to them or because you feel forced, in a sense. The time for settling stops now. Whether it is a friend, lover, or family member, you need to recognize toxicity when you see it. More importantly, learn how to cut it and them out of your life.

Now, you may be saying to yourself, "Cut them out? But what if I love them? What if I want to have a relationship with them?" Yes, there are ways to deal with toxic people. However, we must be mindful of what we give our energy to. If you are consistently trying to salvage a relationship with someone who isn't willing to see the wrong in their actions, you're wasting time that you cannot get back. Yes, some people can change. The question is, are you willing to stick around until they do?

Personally, I've had a fair share of toxic people in my life. For years, I would stay in those friendships and relationships because I didn't want to feel like I was giving them the satisfaction of quitting. I also found myself trying to please others around me, not even realizing that I needed to put my feelings first.

I was in a relationship with someone I knew was taking pleasure in talking to and flirting with other women. I had a family. I didn't want to run. I wanted to try to be the glue to hold us together. After some time had passed, I realized that I, in fact, was the only one trying to do so. Something snapped in me. It was like a bulb went off in my head. I looked in the mirror and thought to myself, "Kita, girl, you are a queen! There are many other people who would love to treat you the way you deserve to be treated. There are others who would cherish every aspect of your being. You have kids to think about and protect." Once I realized I was worth more that what was being handed to me, I walked away and never looked back.

Toxic people are huge hypocrites. They expect you to do what's right, while they continuously cause havoc in your life. They are rude, disrespectful, deceitful, and want their way at any cost. No matter how polite and respectful you are to them, they will not reciprocate those actions because they feel entitled. It's their way or the highway. Going forth, choose to take the highway!

The highway seems like you're giving them what they want. However, let me explain to you what taking the highway means to me.

First, understand what a highway is; a highway is a road that has intersections between them which connects them to different destinations. It has many lanes, which can lead to several different avenues. Now, take that concept and apply it to that toxic relationship you need to break free from. If you decide you'd rather hit the highway, that means you are freeing yourself from a road that was going in a direction that didn't suit you. It's like repetitively driving around a cul-de-sac. You're going in circles and ending up in the same spot. But once you take the road that leads you out of that cul-de-sac, you're able to see the other roads you have been missing out on. I don't want to be restricted. I want to see other avenues. So, when given the option of taking the highway, that'll always be my choice.

Removing yourself from a toxic relationship allows you to see and enjoy things you were once blinded to. You've spent so much time putting up with the storm, you haven't been able to enjoy the rainbow. You've allowed toxicity to get the best of you. How can you tell? You find yourself talking about that toxic person a lot. You dread being around them. You lose control of your temper when you're around them. Most importantly, you begin to stoop to their level, indulging in the same negative behavior. Ask yourself, is it really worth it?

To try to understand why someone is toxic is a task you may never accomplish. They may see something in you that they don't see in themselves. They may envy you. They may admire something about you they could never possess. Whatever the case, it's not for you to continue to try to figure out. Sometimes, people are hurt. As we all should know, hurt people hurt people. Let me say it again. Hurt people hurt people. When someone toxic is going through a painful time, they seek targets to take their frustrations out on. You may be their momentary target. Learn that the battle is with them, not you.

Often, toxic people are hard to deal with because they have enablers. They have people in their lives who, instead of correcting their negative behavior, allow them to continue to be a cancer to those around them. Enablers give toxic people the green light to behave in a condescending manner. If getting rid of the toxic person also means getting rid of the enabler, then be okay with that. When people truly value you, they don't put you in positions to walk away from them. Again, learn to protect your space and sanity.

When you encounter toxicity in your life, learn how to handle it. First, set boundaries and stick to them. Figure out what is not okay with you, and live by that. When a toxic person can no longer break those boundaries, they become powerless.

We've all heard the saying, "Kill them with kindness," right? Just because someone is rude to you doesn't mean you have to reciprocate that same energy. It also doesn't give you an excuse to be rude back. Taking the high road means that you're not allowing their deceitful ways to control your emotions. Smile at them, and keep it moving. If you find it hard to smile at someone who is being condescending, just continue on as if they aren't even in your space. Only a fool argues with himself.

Toxic people expect you to sit there and listen to all of their pessimism. They want you to indulge in pugnacious behavior. Don't spend hours listening to them complain and whine because it will drain you. Toxic people enjoy being the victim. Direct your energy toward those more deserving of it.

Lastly, learn to stand your ground. Toxic people want what they want when they want it. Don't give in. Be firm when dealing with them. Do not allow them to dictate your every move. Once a person can no longer control you, they will try to control how others see you. No worries. If you are a genuine person, no amount of negative backlash can tarnish your character. Those who know the real you won't even humor someone who tries to speak bad on your name.

Toxicity will enter your life for the rest of your life. The goal is not to get even, but to rise above it. Treat toxicity like you do your trash...rid yourself of it.

II.

Too often, we live our lives trying to please others. We do this so much, we lose sight of who we are and what we stand for. We get so caught up in drama and lashing back, we don't stop to see just how much we are missing out on. As mentioned before, every moment wasted is a moment that cannot be recovered. It's time you learn to do you.

In order to become the person you are destined to be, you have to learn to let go of people and situations that weigh you down. A bird cannot fly with a broken wing. The same concept applies to you. You cannot thrive in a circle full of broken, repugnant people. Master the act of preserving your peace. Do you.

Elevation requires separation. Never be afraid to embark on a journey solo. While it's great to have people to share your successes with, know that not everyone will partake in your joys and victories. Learn to separate yourself from those who cannot support you and often find fault in everything you do. Release people who do not accept you for who you are, and are constantly seeking ways to change you. Do you.

Eliminate any situation that is hindering you. Whether it be family, friends, or work, if it is not conducive to the positive lifestyle you are trying to live, then you must rid yourself of it. Make no apologies for the person you yearn to be. Do you.

As much as you may want to seek revenge on someone who has wronged you, don't. Success is the best revenge. People who are trying to pull you down absolutely despise seeing you rise above them. Karma has no deadline. She will make her appearance one way or another, in some shape, form, or fashion. As the wise Wayne Dyer said, "How people treat you is their karma; how you react is yours." Life is like a boomerang. You get back what you put out. Release any anger or resentment you have toward someone. Put great energy into the atmosphere and you will get it back tenfold. Do you.

At the beginning of the year 2019, I created a hashtag for myself: #upwardisthemotion. I continuously live by this. I decided that I will no longer allow my life and emotions be compromised by the deceitful actions of another. My goal is to constantly rise. I do not allow anyone to come and interrupt my happiness. My goal is not to retract, but to excel. I encourage you to do the same. If you are looking back as you walk forward, there is no way you can see what's ahead. Focus on the things that will keep you pushing instead of pulling. Do you.

Simply put, BE ON YOUR SHIT! Stand your ground. Believe in yourself. Ignore anyone or anything that hinders you. Some things in this world are designed to try to pull you to a lower frequency. It's up to you to not allow it. Eradicate obstructive behavior. Don't allow someone to change you to fit their mold of what you should be. Know that you are good enough as you are. Do you!

Chapter Seven

No Fear

I. Find Your Purpose

II. No More Holding Back

I.

How many times have you questioned your existence, asking yourself, "Why am I here? What is my purpose? Will I ever succeed?" Some people are born with purposes that are loud and clear. Maybe they have a specific talent or skill. For others, the answer doesn't come as easy. In order to discover your purpose, you must first define your passion.

Finding yourself requires concentration. You have a purpose. Everyone does. It is within you. It is not something you have to try to create, only uncover. Unearthing your passion means discovering something you absolutely love doing. Think of what it is you do that comes fairly simple to you. Of course, even the best artists, actors, and musicians have to practice in order to perfect their craft, just as you will. But whatever craft they have soothes their soul, puts them at ease, and makes them happy. Maybe you are good at leading people. Perhaps you are very talented at sculpting. No matter what you do, you will always have to work hard. Be that as it may, working hard and fulfilling your passion will not feel forced. If you do not feel a sense of joy, blessedness, and peace of mind while developing your passion and purpose, then you have not yet discovered it.

Ask yourself... what things do you take pleasure in? What qualities do you possess that you adore sharing with others? How could others benefit from your passion? How can you benefit from your purpose? Do you find solitude in helping others? Can you make the world a better place? Can you make someone's life more sustainable? These are questions that can and will help you on your journey of self-discovery, which will lead you to your passion and purpose.

Set aside time to gain clarity on your purpose. In that time, think really hard about the things that bring you immense bliss. Reflect on where you are in life and what you want to do with it. Are you satisfied financially? Are you in good health? Where would you like to reside? What kind of career do you really want? Once you figure out what your goals are, put it out to the universe.

We have to learn to follow our hearts. When you are connected to a happier you, your soul feels at ease, and you become inspired. Our heart is what keeps us alive. Without it, we are nothing. It is detrimental to our survival, so why not use our most powerful bodily resource to help us discover our purpose? You can think of a million things you may be good at, but what is your heart telling you? When you ponder about that moment you won a talent show, does your heart skip a beat? When you remember the time you achieved a first-place certificate for that writing contest, do you feel flutters? When you think of the moment you completed your first stage play, and received standing ovations, do you feel overwhelmed with joy? These are moments you should be living for. These are the moments which will lead you to your purpose in life.

Find out what invigorates you. So often, we drain ourselves by putting all of our energy into the wrong things, the very things that will not lead us to our destiny. When I worked in retail, I would absolutely despise having to deal with so many angry people. I would go into work unhappy and leave even more unhappy. By the time I got home, I had little to no drive left to focus on the tasks that actually gave me a sense of purpose. It was then that I realized giving my energy to the wrong things were pulling me away from the blessings God had in store for me. As mentioned before, the goal is to focus on what will keep you pushing instead of pulling.

When you are trying to discover your purpose, you have to be clear on the things you are willing to sacrifice. This could mean losing some people along the way. In chapter six, we mentioned how elevation requires separation. Not everyone is meant to go where you are headed. When you become serious about your aspirations, and begin to focus solely on completing whatever it will take to get you there, you will receive backlash from those you least expect. You will lose friends and possibly fall out with a few family members. They will concoct the notion that you think you're better than them. They will accuse you of being fake, possibly even selfish. They will talk down on you to others. They will begin to smear your name. And, before you know it, you will find yourself defending your integrity. The astute T.D Jakes said, "Rather than defending yourself or your integrity, just keep doing what you're doing." Don't worry about who you will lose along the way. If losing someone means finding yourself, then so be it.

Along with losing people throughout your journey of self-discovery, you will also forfeit other elements. You will have sleepless nights and restless days. You will have to invest. You will have to sacrifice a few nights out with friends. This is all a part of growth. If you are serious about finding your purpose, you will do what it takes, no excuses.

To find your purpose means to find yourself. Life is not about feeling stuck, but breaking free from all things that bind us. Your purpose is the reason you get up every morning. Get uncomfortable and step outside of the bubble you put yourself in. Stop procrastinating due to fear of failure. Tie your existence to your purpose and live the life God intended for you to live.

II.

I read a book, by Steve Harvey, titled *Jump,* and it really had me thinking. In his book, he speaks of not being afraid to jump into the life you desire. With every word I read, I realized just how much I was holding myself back from utilizing my God given talents, merely because I was afraid that it would lead to nowhere. That is, until I decided to take a gamble on myself.

For years, I have always loved to write. I found myself doing so at the best and worst times of my life. It didn't have to be anything specific to write about. I just did it whenever it tickled my fancy. I would write about school, friends, my daily tasks, or whatever crossed my mind. I remember writing a story, when I was in fifth grade, and to my surprise, my teacher loved it. Her feedback gave me an inkling of what I wanted to do with my life.

As the years rolled by, I still wrote. However, I did not bring any of it to the forefront because people always talked about how a steady stream of income was the determining factor in being able to take care of myself and pay my bills. So, after graduating high school, I decided to go away to college for nursing. Subsequent to me getting pregnant with my oldest son, I dropped out and headed back home.

Years later, I enrolled in another college to complete what I had started. Again, I did not finish. Although I knew that a nurse's salary would take care of me and my family, I just didn't have the drive to become one. While trying to obtain my nursing degree, I had a writing class. I did so well with all of my papers, my instructor couldn't understand why I wasn't pursing a degree in journalism, or something of the sort. When I was in that class, I felt alive. I put my all into every paper I was assigned, receiving nothing less than an A- on each one.

More time had passed. Still, here I was trying to force myself to work jobs I had no desire for. I even went back to school for pharmacy. Nope...didn't finish that either. I would always have excuses as to why I did not follow through. In a sense, I was trying to trick myself into believing what I was saying was true.

One day, after sitting around feeling a sense of failure, I picked up a pen and paper and started writing down all the things I wanted to change in my life. As I was writing, I stopped mid-sentence. I realized I was doing the very thing which kept me feeling alive. I was writing. I decided that although money was key in survival, so was happiness. I told myself I was going to write my first book. I had no clue how to go about it or get it printed, but that did not stop me. I wrote morning, noon, and night. I did research on how to structure my book and how to get my ISBN. I looked up how to retrieve a barcode and get my book printed. I found out how to get it on Amazon and other avenues. And, in March of 2018, I released my first book, *Twisted Devotion.*

This accomplishment may not seem like anything to lots of people, but it meant everything to me. I felt a sense of consummation. I smashed a lifetime goal. I put my energy into the very thing people said would lead me nowhere. Funny thing is, I did not do it for monetary gain. I did it because it fulfilled me. It made me feel whole. It gave me life. It was something I could look back on and be proud of.

When you are doing what you love, you won't focus on currency. Yes, I made some money off my book, but that didn't compare to the joys I felt when I received good feedback from it. Of course, with it being my first book, there was definitely room for improvement. That comes with anything. But to be able to finally do something I love was worth more than anything.

Often times, we worry about how we are going to survive if we quit our jobs. We tend to wonder how we will take care of ourselves, our family, and our bills. Because of this, we stay stuck in our dejected circumstances. We run ourselves to the ground for jobs that won't think twice about replacing us before our seats get cold. We spend hours on end working to make others wealthy, while we wallow in misery. We inadvertently neglect our children. The time for that stops now.

You are the only person who can change your life. When will you start? When will you begin to look out for you? When will you stop boxing yourself in? When will you jump over those hurdles in your life? When will your procrastination cease? When will you grasp the concept that you are your biggest challenge? When will you understand that you have a purpose in life? When will you let go of the notion that you have to fit the mold instead of recognizing the fact that you were born to stand out?

Learn to step out on faith. Believe in yourself and your capabilities. Stop being afraid of what MAY happen and think of the endless, optimistic possibilities that COULD happen. Do not allow fear to run your life or ruin it. No more holding yourself back. If you believe in a higher power, then you know that your destiny is covered. Manifest a life of prosperity. Seek an abundance of happiness. Surmount any challenges you face instead of running from them. STOP BEING AFRAID. The life you deserve is waiting for you. Go and get it, now.

Chapter Eight

Omega

I. Setbacks

II. Out with The Old

I.

How many times have you attempted to complete a goal only to find yourself back at square one? You promised yourself you would start working out, but couldn't because you developed a knee injury. You enrolled in classes, but you can no longer go because your scholarship fell through. You bought supplies to renovate your bathroom, but now you can't because your hot water heater went out and you have to replace it. You made plans to attend an important conference, but now you have to miss it because your tire blew on the way there. You were getting ready to purchase yourself a brand-new car, but you weren't able to because a new, negative inquiry popped up on your credit report, so now you need a co-signer. Before you know it, you are just about ready to throw in the towel.

Setbacks are a natural part of life. It happens to the best of us. It seems to occur at the most detrimental times in our lives. The key to getting through a setback is knowing it is just that, a setback. Delayed is not denied. It does not mean your goal is no longer attainable. It means you have to get yourself through your setback so you can continue to thrive.

When going through a setback, one of the first things you need to do is acknowledge it. Accept that a roadblock has occurred. You cannot pretend that it didn't happen. And you don't have to hide your emotions about it. It is okay to feel anger. Understand that setbacks are innate. It doesn't just happen to certain people; it happens to everyone. You are not exempt. Acknowledging the issue will allow you to process it, thus creating a platform for you to move past it.

Next, you need to reflect on what went wrong. Think about your initial goal. What, doing your journey, did not go as you envisioned? Were you given a sign that you ignored? Did you take bad advice? How did you end up in a temporary rut? Asking yourself these questions is essential when trying to devise a plan to go forth. You cannot fix the situation if you don't know exactly where it went south. The goal is to avoid another setback.

When reflecting on what went wrong, refrain from feeling like a failure. Again, setbacks happen to us all. It does not mean you lack the skills to be able to smash your goal. It does not mean your dream isn't meant for you. Don't spend valuable time dwelling on what has happened. You can no longer change it. Do not victimize yourself. Instead of beating yourself up about it and feeling sorry for yourself, know that you will make it through. Consider it a minor setback for a major comeback. You will be just fine.

During this process, you must allow yourself time to heal. Stop feeling like you have to rush back into the swing of things. Healing is significant during a setback. Impatience will only hinder you. If you break your leg, there's no possible way you will be able to walk on it without causing more pain and damage, right? Your bone has to mend itself and become strong again. So, why wouldn't the same concept apply to your emotional and mental being? Allow yourself time to become whole again. Half of you isn't going to get the job done. Sorry.

While solitude is good in some ways, it isn't in others. When going through a rough patch, surround yourself with positive people, for it is imperative that you stay lifted during this time. You don't need anyone around you who cannot offer genuine words of encouragement. They will only hamper the process. At this vulnerable time, you need to be encompassed by good vibes only. A strong support system will provide you with the motivation necessary to get through your trials and tribulations. You require a drama free zone, a zone full of irrefutable motivation and influences.

Learning from your setback is mandatory. If you don't learn from what hindered you, how can you ever move forward from it? Experience is the best teacher. Failure opens the doorway for you to become better at your craft. While it may be an expensive price to pay, it will equip you with the tools needed to be successful. It is merely a stepping stone to get to where you desire to be. So, embrace it.

Lastly, follow through! You didn't make it as far as you did just to allow a setback to stop you. Reclaim your life and take back control of what belongs to you. Set aside any fears and get back on track. Revisit your initial goals and put forth the effort to bring them to life again. Revise your plan, set a strategy, and stick with it. Take all the time necessary; make it be on your side. Remember, a goal without a plan is a disaster waiting to happen. Now that you've survived your setback, go be great!

II.

Quite often, when we go through hard times, we try to trick our minds into believing that we are okay after a while. We do things to stay busy. We lean to our support system. We even give ourselves pep talks...confirmation that we are, indeed, alright. Truth is, we still find ourselves feeling a sense of melancholy. You sit there trying to piece the puzzle together. You finally landed a new job, you lost that fifteen pounds that lingered on to you, and you even broke up with your mate because you weren't being treated the correct way. So, why do you still feel like a dark cloud is still wavering over your head? You did not break up with the old you.

Imagine breaking up with someone you once loved, who hurt you tremendously, but never ridding yourself of memories associated with that person. You still hang on to that picture of you two from your boat cruise. You still sleep next to that giant teddy bear he won for you at the festival. You still use the same cologne your mate bought you for your birthday. You still read through all of the old text messages between the two of you. Yet, you wonder why you still feel unhappy during the time you should be happy most. Why are you holding on to things affiliated with events or people that are now a part of your past?

During those transitions, you must break up with who you were at that time in your life. Leaving those memories behind means leaving that version of yourself behind as well. You cannot step into a new you if you're carrying old baggage. The goal is to become a better version of yourself, not a bitter version. Sure, there's no possible way to completely forget everything about something or someone. However, acknowledging and leaving those painful memories behind only means you are on a quest to find the new you. That is the goal, right?

Don't be afraid to declutter your life. It is no longer about the person you once were. It's about the person you desire to be, a better you. Understand that the power is in your hands. You are responsible for recognizing your worth. You hold the key to your happiness. You have to be the one to know you are magnificent. You are the one who must be unapologetic for deciding to change your life for the better. If you want a life of peace and joy, you must create it. You, you, you!

Don't be afraid to take risks. Hop out there and go for it. Stop playing it safe all the damn time. You will never know how far you can go if you don't try. Go for that higher position at work. Better yet, start your own company just as you planned to do years ago. Join that gym and get healthy and in shape, for yourself. Be bold and enter that poetry contest. Sign up for cosmetology school. Cut your long hair off. Move to another state. Dismiss that negative friend you felt obligated to be around. Break up with the old you so that you can create the new you. Whatever it will take to help you become a better version of yourself, do it!

Understand that anything worth having isn't coming easy. You have to be willing to put in work. You spend so much time making sure your house is spotless, your car is squeaky clean, the family is taken care of, and your yard is impeccable. Yet, you constantly put off what needs to be done regarding yourself and your well-being. You matter as well! While you're out there watering your grass, water your soul. No, you won't wake up and be a different person in one day. Treat yourself like a construction site for a new building; develop a blueprint and slowly build.

The ball is in your court. So, what will you do with it? The clock is constantly ticking. Are you going to let another few years go by before you decide to give yourself the life you deserve? Or, will you begin to change your life in order to become a better version of yourself? The answer lies in you.

In high school, I had a teacher who used to tell it like it was. He did not hold back how he was feeling. Mr. Boughton would come off like a jerk at times, but most kids in my school had mad admiration for him because he did not tolerate anything other than respect. He continuously said something to students that will forever stay with me. He would look at them and say, "You're a fastidious entity with a propensity toward procrastination!" Mr. Boughton knew that each and every one of us had potential, but that we got in our own way of success. He saw something in us we couldn't completely see in ourselves. He knew we had the tools to thrive, just as I know you do.

In no way do I profess to be a psychologist. I am merely sharing my knowledge with you in hopes of you becoming the person you need to be, having the wonderful life you deserve. Do not wait another precious moment procrastinating. No more putting off what needs to be done.

I will never forget a moment I shared with my aunt, many years ago, before she passed away of cancer. She was lying down, in her hospital bed, while my cousin Brian and I sat in her room. It was quiet. We were sad because we knew she would not be with us much longer. She saw the broken-heartedness on our faces. She looked at me, then at Brian. In a faint voice, she said, "What's wrong, Brian? Somebody messing with you? 'Cause you know I'll jack 'em up for you." Brian smiled through his pain, and so did I.

There I was, watching someone I loved dearly try to put a smile on our faces despite the agony and pain she felt. She fought all the way to the end. I realized that if she could find the strength to fight and be courageous, then what was my excuse? Thank you, Auntie Linda. You helped me more than you will ever know. I love you, eternally.

Find yourself, passion, and purpose. Know that you can achieve anything. The sky is the limit. Going forth, live with no regrets. Always remember that you are deserving. No more putting off for tomorrow what needs to be done today. Devise a plan and stick to it. Be done with anyone or anything that is not conducive to the life you yearn. I believe in you, but you must believe in yourself. After all, it's about rejuvenation. Go to the nearest mirror, look in it, and promise to become a better version of yourself!

You can follow the author on her social media sites:

Facebook

Kita Lashaun

Instagram

Kita_Lashaun

Feel free to also visit the website, www.openmicproduction.net, where you can find her podcast and other projects she has done relating to Open Mic Production.

*Do what you love, and love what you do.
Never allow anyone to put a title on you.*

Kita LaShaun

www.ingramcontent.com/pod-product-compliance
Lightning Source LLC
Chambersburg PA
CBHW051842040426
42447CB00006B/651